COMING HOME

MAPPING AND SHAPING YOUR AUTONOMIC NERVOUS SYSTEM

©DANIEL MORRISON 2021

WWW.QCHANGES.CO.UK

Acknowledgements

This work is based on research carried out by Dr. Stephen Porges into polyvagal theory, and work by Deb Dana on the application of polyvagal theory in therapy.

This journal accompanies Coming Home, a workshop by Q Changes.

Welcome!

Have you ever reacted in a way that wasn't appropriate to the situation?

Have you ever been flooded with emotion for no reason?

Have you ever felt that things are suddenly not ok, although nothing has changed?

Your autonomic nervous system is always working in service of your survival. It constantly asks the question, am I safe? It sends a stream of information to your brain, operating below the level of conscious awareness.

By learning to notice and name these patterns, you can become the active operator of your system. You can understand how to experience safety and what cues of danger take you into a state of protection.

We all have a home in a ventral state of belonging and connection. We might have been lost for years, or only visited briefly, but we can all learn the way home.

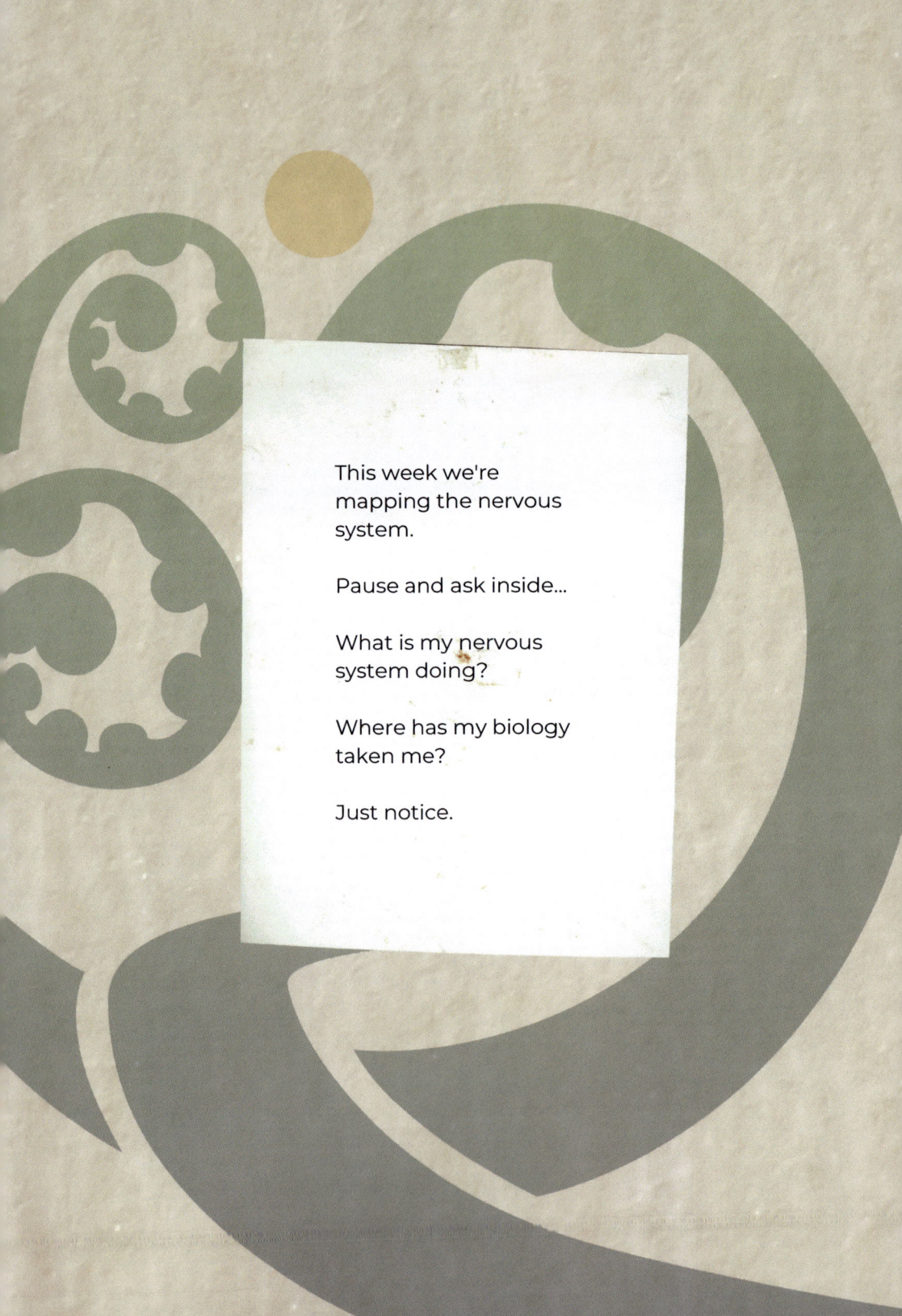

This week we're mapping the nervous system.

Pause and ask inside...

What is my nervous system doing?

Where has my biology taken me?

Just notice.

Mapping

Ventral Vagal

Sympathetic

Dorsal Vagal

WEEK ONE: Mapping

Ventral Vagal

I am....

The world is....

Sympathetic Arousal

I am...

The world is...

Dorsal Vagal

I am...

The world is...

What's your intention for the week? How often will you check in?

How will you remind yourself to pause and ask inside?

How do you feel about this intention?

DATE:

Where has your biology taken you today?

Can you track the shifts?

DATE:

Where has your biology taken you today?

Can you track the shifts?

DATE:

Where has your biology taken you today?

Can you track the shifts?

DATE:

Where has your biology taken you today?

Can you track the shifts?

DATE:

Where has your biology taken you today?

Can you track the shifts?

DATE:

Where has your biology taken you today?

Can you track the shifts?

DATE:

Where has your biology taken you today?

Can you track the shifts?

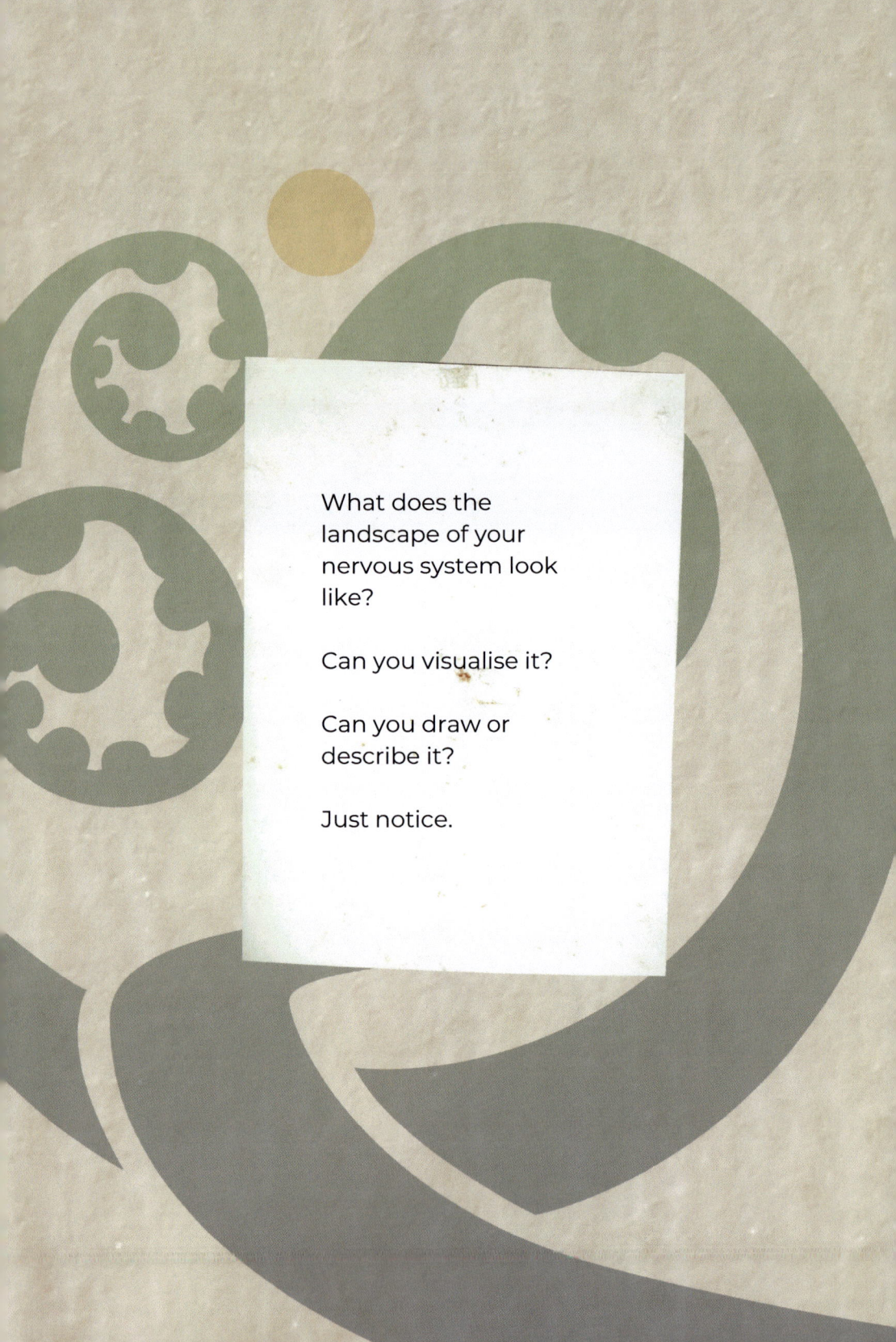

What does the landscape of your nervous system look like?

Can you visualise it?

Can you draw or describe it?

Just notice.

Exploring the Landscape

Ventral Vagal

Sympathetic

Dorsal Vagal

WEEK TWO: Exploring the Landscape

How does your nervous system send you a 'YES'?

How does your nervous system send you a 'NO'?

What words work for you?
It's my biology sending me a message.
All I have to do is notice and name it.
I can listen and turn towards without judging.
……

What's your intention for the week? How often will you check in?

How will you remind yourself to pause and ask inside?

How do you feel about this intention?

DATE:

Where has your biology taken you today?

Can you track the shifts?

DATE:

Where has your biology taken you today?

Can you track the shifts?

DATE:

Where has your biology taken you today?

Can you track the shifts?

DATE:

Where has your biology taken you today?

Can you track the shifts?

DATE:

Where has your biology taken you today?

Can you track the shifts?

DATE:

Where has your biology taken you today?

Can you track the shifts?

DATE:

Where has your biology taken you today?

Can you track the shifts?

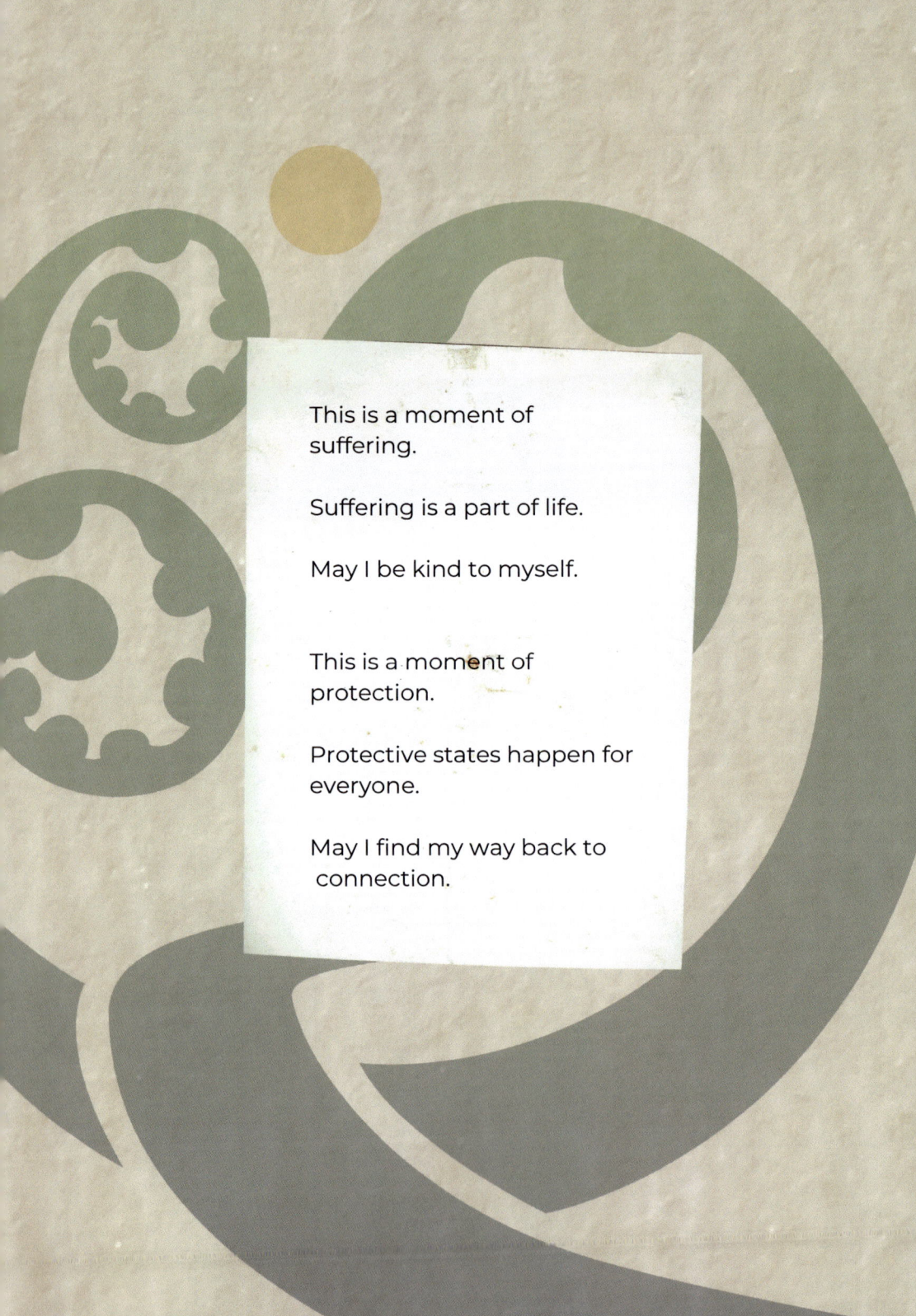

This is a moment of suffering.

Suffering is a part of life.

May I be kind to myself.

This is a moment of protection.

Protective states happen for everyone.

May I find my way back to connection.

WEEK THREE: Triggers and Glimmers

What triggers can you notice from the last week?

Are there any you can anticipate in the next week?

What glimmers do you remember from the last week?

Are there any you can anticipate in the next week?

What's your intention for the week? How often will you check in?

How will you remind yourself to pause and ask inside?

How do you feel about this intention?

DATE:

What triggers and glimmers have you noticed today?

Where has your biology taken you today?

Can you track the shifts?

DATE:

What triggers and glimmers have you noticed today?

Where has your biology taken you today?

Can you track the shifts?

DATE:

What triggers and glimmers have you noticed today?

Where has your biology taken you today?

Can you track the shifts?

DATE:

What triggers and glimmers have you noticed today?

Where has your biology taken you today?

Can you track the shifts?

DATE:

What triggers and glimmers have you noticed today?

Where has your biology taken you today?

Can you track the shifts?

DATE:

What triggers and glimmers have you noticed today?

Where has your biology taken you today?

Can you track the shifts?

DATE:

What triggers and glimmers have you noticed today?

Where has your biology taken you today?

Can you track the shifts?

Dr. Stephen Porges said that the lifetime aim of the autonomic nervous system is to feel safe in the arms of an appropriate mammal.

We're designed for co-regulation.

How do you regulate your system with others?

What can you do alone to regulate your system?

I'm so .... I could ....

Just like me ......

WEEK FOUR: Regulating Resources

What's your image of fullness or emptiness?

How does your nervous system let you know?

What's your intention for the week? How often will you check in?

How will you remind yourself to pause and ask inside?

How do you feel about this intention?

DATE:

What has filled you today?

What has drained you?

What have you savoured today?

Where has your biology taken you?

Can you track the shifts?

DATE:

What has filled you today?

What has drained you?

What have you savoured today?

Where has your biology taken you?

Can you track the shifts?

DATE:

What has filled you today?

What has drained you?

What have you savoured today?

Where has your biology taken you?

Can you track the shifts?

DATE:

What has filled you today?

What has drained you?

What have you savoured today?

Where has your biology taken you?

Can you track the shifts?

DATE:

What has filled you today?

What has drained you?

What have you savoured today?

Where has your biology taken you?

Can you track the shifts?

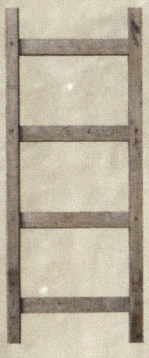

DATE:

What has filled you today?

What has drained you?

What have you savoured today?

Where has your biology taken you?

Can you track the shifts?

DATE:

What has filled you today?

What has drained you?

What have you savoured today?

Where has your biology taken you?

Can you track the shifts?

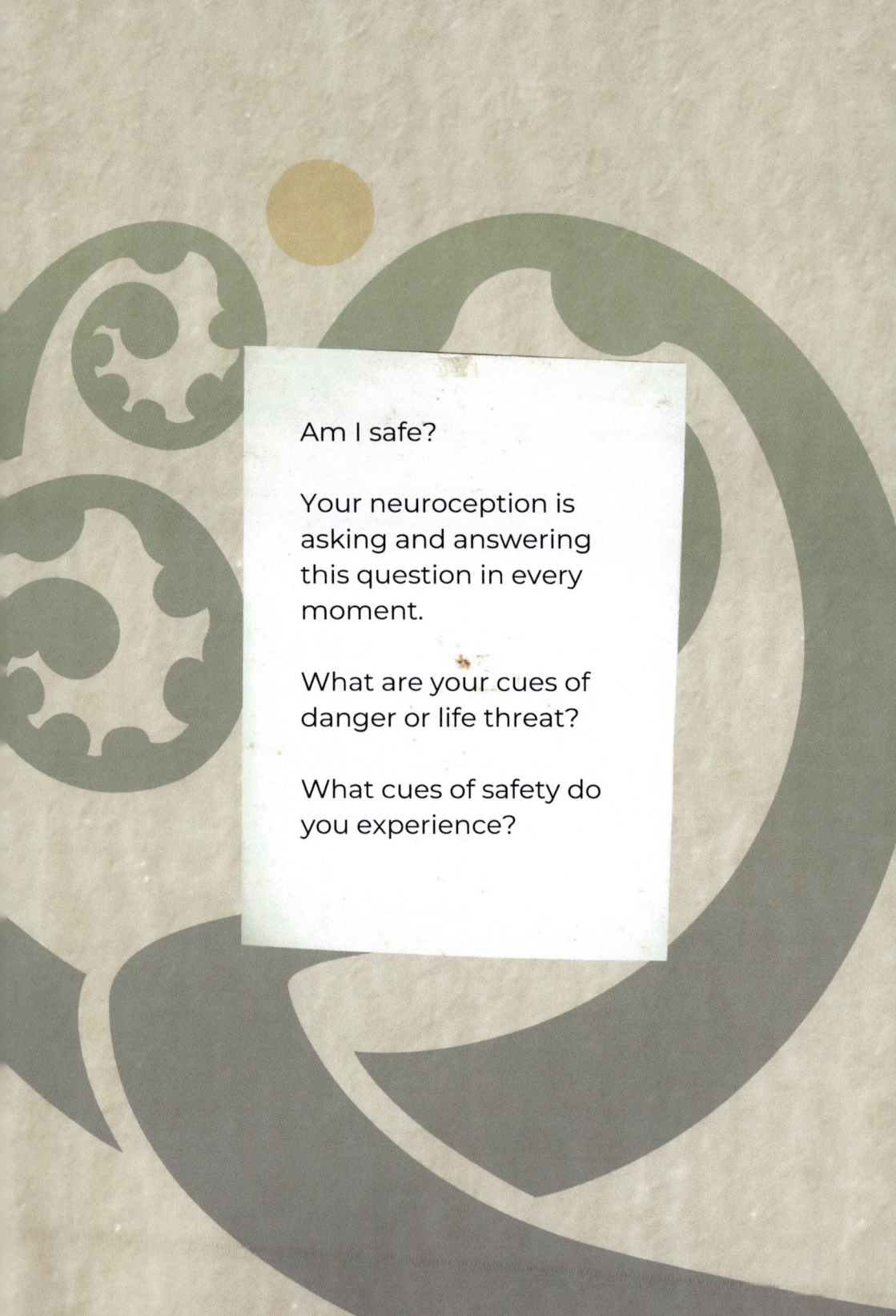

Am I safe?

Your neuroception is asking and answering this question in every moment.

What are your cues of danger or life threat?

What cues of safety do you experience?

WEEK FIVE: Neuroception

What's your image of your autonomic surveillance system?

What embodied cues are you receiving right now, from inside?

What environmental cues are you receiving right now, from outside?

What interpersonal cues is your social engagement system receiving right now?

What's your intention for the week? How often will you check in?

How will you remind yourself to pause and ask inside?

How do you feel about this intention?

DATE:

What embodied cues have you noticed today?

What environmental cues have you noticed?

What interpersonal cues has your social engagement system received?

What states has your biology taken you to today?

Can you track the shifts?

DATE:

What embodied cues have you noticed today?

What environmental cues have you noticed?

What interpersonal cues has your social engagement system received?

What states has your biology taken you to today?

Can you track the shifts?

DATE:

What embodied cues have you noticed today?

What environmental cues have you noticed?

What interpersonal cues has your social engagement system received?

What states has your biology taken you to today?

Can you track the shifts?

DATE:

What embodied cues have you noticed today?

What environmental cues have you noticed?

What interpersonal cues has your social engagement system received?

What states has your biology taken you to today?

Can you track the shifts?

DATE:

What embodied cues have you noticed today?

What environmental cues have you noticed?

What interpersonal cues has your social engagement system received?

What states has your biology taken you to today?

Can you track the shifts?

DATE:

What embodied cues have you noticed today?

What environmental cues have you noticed?

What interpersonal cues has your social engagement system received?

What states has your biology taken you to today?

Can you track the shifts?

DATE:

What embodied cues have you noticed today?

What environmental cues have you noticed?

What interpersonal cues has your social engagement system received?

What states has your biology taken you to today?

Can you track the shifts?

When we see actions are based in our biology, we can sense that the only autonomic intention is survival.

We all have a home in ventral and a home away from home.

Can you look at your home away from home and feel how it has sheltered and protected you?

My Patterns

Sympathetic Arousal States

Fight Indicators

I am often angry
I can be assertive if I need to
I tend to bully others
I control situations to feel safe
I am good at boundaries
I can draw on courage
I can lead if needed
People are scared of me
I challenge injustices
I am always right
I take what I want
I can express my wants

Sympathetic Arousal States

Flight Indicators

I am often rushing around
I have energy to draw upon
I can work hard when needed
I often worry
I can keep going when I have to
I avoid feeling
I can leave when necessary
I'm always so busy
I can contain feelings appropriately
I am a human doing
I can get a job done

Sympathetic Arousal States

Freeze Indicators

I often space out
I can switch off when I need to
I don't interrupt others
I feel like I'm hiding
I can be still when others panic
I feel small
Relationships aren't safe
I don't make a bad situation worse
I feel like giving up
I sit around all day
I am good at being on my own
I am motivated to meditate

Sympathetic Arousal States

Fawn Indicators

I am always pleasing others
I am attentive to my lover
I will help others where needed
I am afraid to say no
I lose myself in others
I can listen when it's needed
I value fairness
I fear what others think of me
I rarely reveal my true desires
I value fairness
I keep the peace in tricky moments
I give to feel safe
I am a good therapist

WEEK SIX: Patterns of Connection and Protection

Where is your home away from home?

How has it taken care of you?

Can you map a pattern with a loved one?

What does your mechanism of movement look like?

What's your intention for the week? How often will you check in?

How will you remind yourself to pause and ask inside?

How do you feel about this intention?

DATE:

What patterns have you noticed today?

Where has your biology taken you today?

Can you track the shifts?

DATE:

What patterns have you noticed today?

Where has your biology taken you today?

Can you track the shifts?

DATE:

What patterns have you noticed today?

Where has your biology taken you today?

Can you track the shifts?

DATE:

What patterns have you noticed today?

Where has your biology taken you today?

Can you track the shifts?

DATE:

What patterns have you noticed today?

Where has your biology taken you today?

Can you track the shifts?

DATE:

What patterns have you noticed today?

Where has your biology taken you today?

Can you track the shifts?

DATE:

What patterns have you noticed today?

Where has your biology taken you today?

Can you track the shifts?

Story follows state.

We view the world around us through the lens of our current state.

Thing of a story, an incident, a situation in your life.

How does it change?

Can you bring curiosity and compassion to it?

My Stories

WEEK SEVEN: Story Follows State

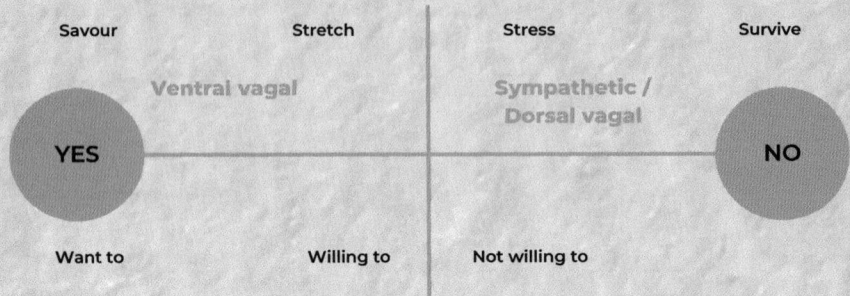

How will you recognise this line? What images, words or body sensations will your nervous system send you?

What's your intention for the week? How often will you check in?

How will you remind yourself to pause and ask inside?

How do you feel about this intention?

DATE:

What stories have you noticed today?

Can you be curious about the possibility of a different story?

Do you feel an autonomic yes or no to this story? Can you change it again?

Where has your biology taken you today?

Can you track the shifts?

DATE:

What stories have you noticed today?

Can you be curious about the possibility of a different story?

Do you feel an autonomic yes or no to this story? Can you change it again?

Where has your biology taken you today?

Can you track the shifts?

DATE:

What stories have you noticed today?

Can you be curious about the possibility of a different story?

Do you feel an autonomic yes or no to this story? Can you change it again?

Where has your biology taken you today?

Can you track the shifts?

DATE:

What stories have you noticed today?

Can you be curious about the possibility of a different story?

Do you feel an autonomic yes or no to this story? Can you change it again?

Where has your biology taken you today?

Can you track the shifts?

DATE:

What stories have you noticed today?

Can you be curious about the possibility of a different story?

Do you feel an autonomic yes or no to this story? Can you change it again?

Where has your biology taken you today?

Can you track the shifts?

DATE:

What stories have you noticed today?

Can you be curious about the possibility of a different story?

Do you feel an autonomic yes or no to this story? Can you change it again?

Where has your biology taken you today?

Can you track the shifts?

DATE:

What stories have you noticed today?

Can you be curious about the possibility of a different story?

Do you feel an autonomic yes or no to this story? Can you change it again?

Where has your biology taken you today?

Can you track the shifts?

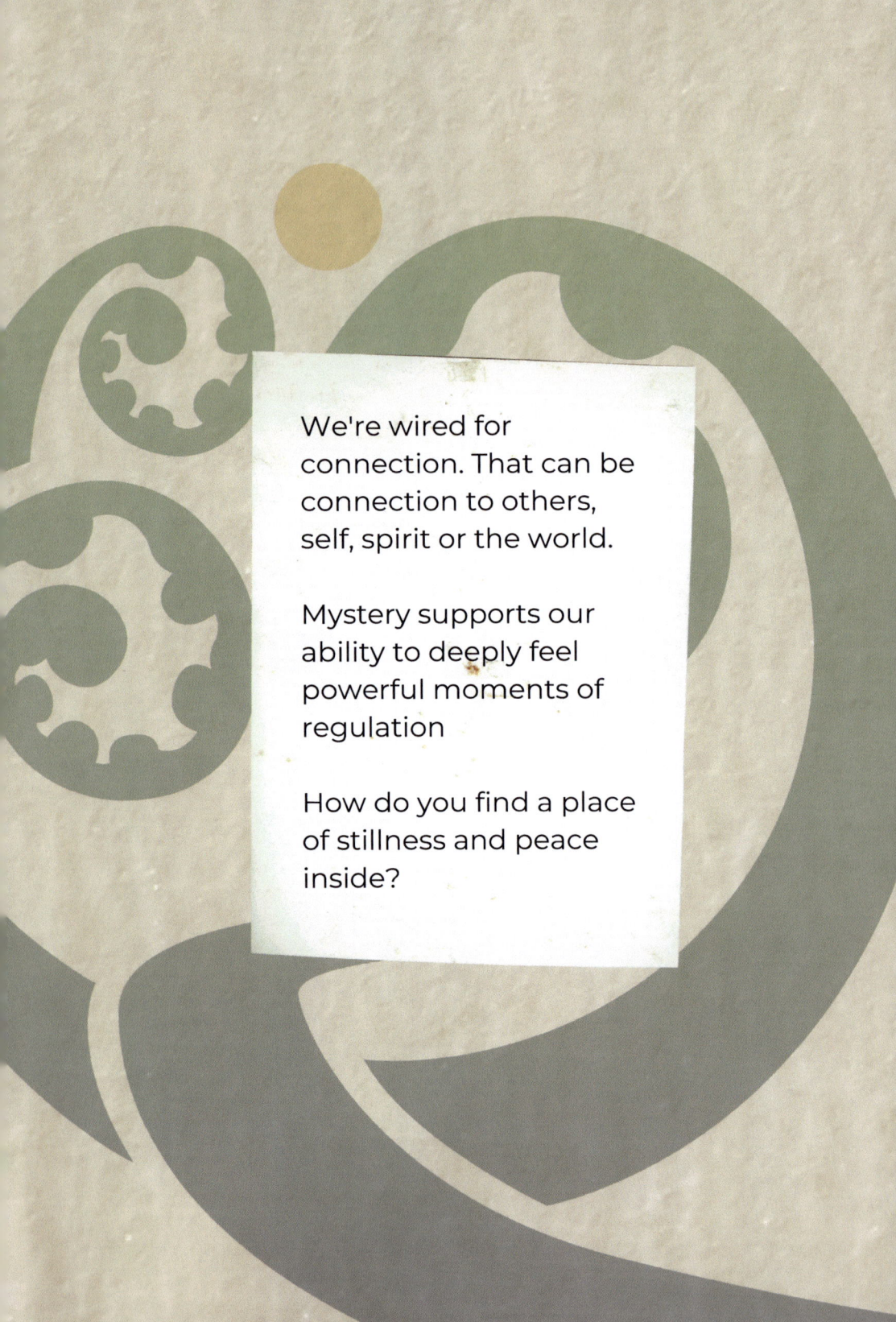

We're wired for connection. That can be connection to others, self, spirit or the world.

Mystery supports our ability to deeply feel powerful moments of regulation

How do you find a place of stillness and peace inside?

Connection to...

- Spirit
- The World
- Others
- Self

WEEK EIGHT: Transcendent Experiences

What deeply nourishing moments can you remember?

How does your nervous system react to stillness?

What one thing do you want to remember from this course?

Do you have an ongoing intention to continue this practice?

What's your intention for the week? How often will you check in?

How will you remind yourself to pause and ask inside?

DATE:

What have you practised from the course today?

Where has your biology taken you?

Can you track the shifts?

DATE:

What have you practised from the course today?

Where has your biology taken you?

Can you track the shifts?

DATE:

What have you practised from the course today?

Where has your biology taken you?

Can you track the shifts?

DATE:

What have you practised from the course today?

Where has your biology taken you?

Can you track the shifts?

DATE:

What have you practised from the course today?

Where has your biology taken you?

Can you track the shifts?

DATE:

What have you practised from the course today?

Where has your biology taken you?

Can you track the shifts?

DATE:

What have you practised from the course today?

Where has your biology taken you?

Can you track the shifts?

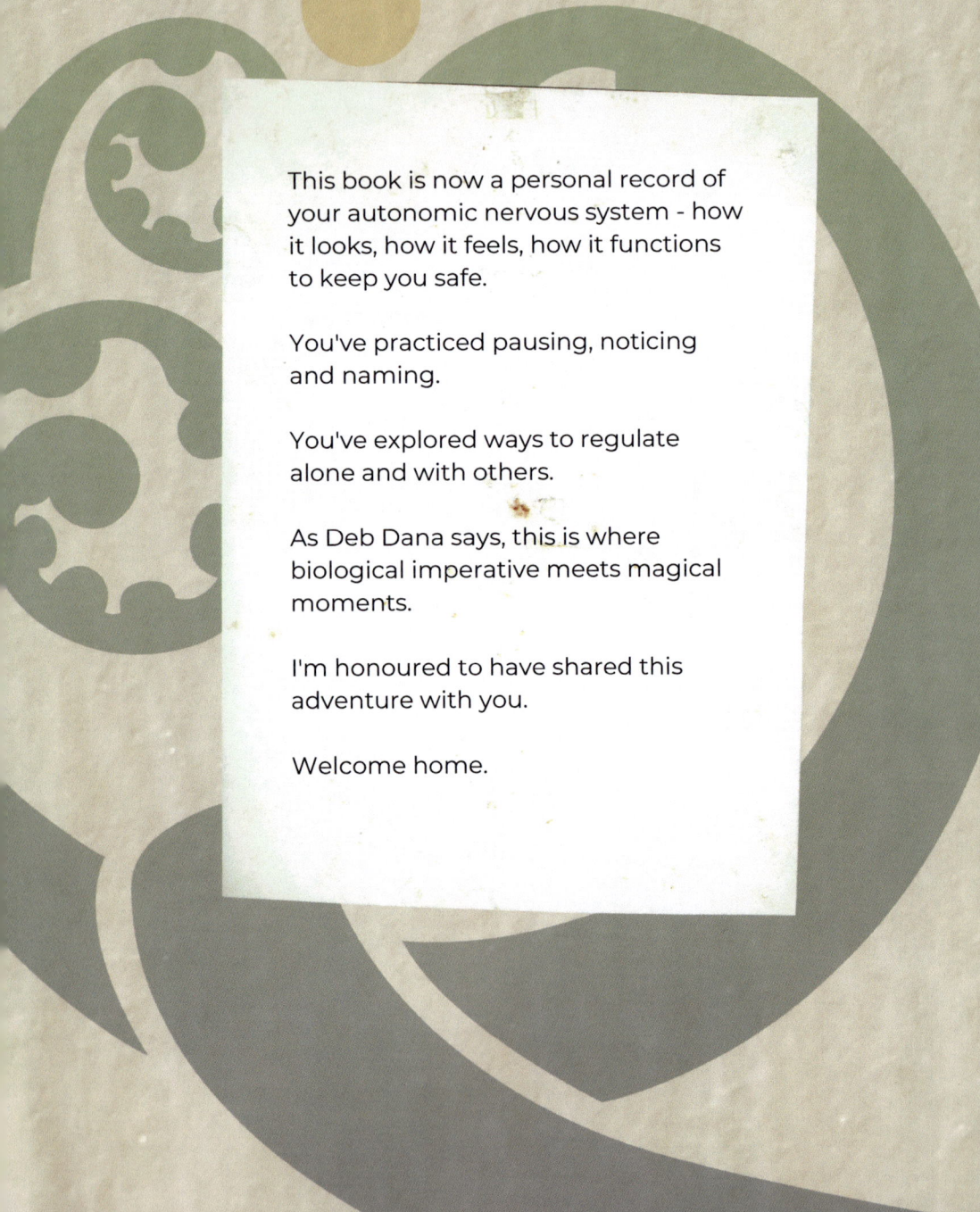

This book is now a personal record of your autonomic nervous system - how it looks, how it feels, how it functions to keep you safe.

You've practiced pausing, noticing and naming.

You've explored ways to regulate alone and with others.

As Deb Dana says, this is where biological imperative meets magical moments.

I'm honoured to have shared this adventure with you.

Welcome home.

If you'd like to explore this more deeply, Deb Dana's audiobook is excellent. It's called Befriending your Nervous System and is available on Audible.

If you want to know more about the research behind this work, take a look at The Polyvagal Theory: Neurophysiological Foundations of Emotions, Attachment, Communication and Self-Regulation by Dr Stephen Porges, published by Norton.

For more workshops from us, see www.qchanges.co.uk

Other great workshops can be found at artofconsent.co.uk and trueselfsystems.com

Am I safe?

Ventral Vagal — Safe, Connected

Sympathetic — Energised, Excited → **Dorsal Vagal** — Resting, Digesting

Sympathetic — Fight, Flight, Freeze → **Dorsal Vagal** — Flop, Shutdown

Things to remember...

Things to remember...

Things to remember...

Things to remember...

Printed in Great Britain
by Amazon